Less

Than

Perfect

By Patrick J. Doty

Edited by Sally Stopper

Brookside Publishing

115 Brook Avenue, Atlantic Highlands, NJ 07716

ISBN: 978-0-9886467-1-1
eISBN: 978-0-9886467-0-4

10 9 8 7 6 5 4 3 2 1

The Pat I Never Knew

From the Editor

My daily life is filled with people. Sometimes there is a brief exchange, but mostly they just pass by. I usually take no notice as I hurry through my day. This will no longer be the case. My chance encounter with this author has changed me... improved me. He has a calming, positive outlook and a genuine compassion and tolerance for all people. He is not a shoulder to cry on, but can be a shoulder to lean on. I strive to live by the example of my treasured friend and thank God I didn't let this one "just pass by". He may be Less Than Perfect, but not when it matters most.

The truth is, I grew up living next door to Patrick Doty.....right next door. I have known of him for more than 40 years. He was a "bad kid" and I never had anything to do with him. When he sent me a friend request on Facebook two years ago, I shuddered. "What the hell does HE want"? His family had moved away almost 30 years ago and I had all but forgotten him. I reminded myself that people can change, and opened up a conversation with him. I was immediately taken in by his infectious sense of fun and humor, and of course, his storytelling. At the time, he was a contractor for kitchen and bath renovations. In the course of one of our regular chats, he told me that he had always wanted to write

1

the story of his life. Neither of us had any experience with this, but I offered to be his editor and he began writing immediately.

Almost everyone says they want to write the story of their life, but most never do. I had no expectations beyond a few weeks. He wrote a few chapters and I went to work on them. Not knowing much about his past, I wasn't prepared for the stories that started to flow. Some made me smile, some made me cry, and others gave me a guilty thrill.

It has been a privilege for me to be involved with this book. Pat has a sincere and heartfelt desire to help others by showing them that they are not alone and proving that, even in the most difficult of life's situations, there is light.

Take time to notice the people who cross your path every day. Never dismiss the opportunity to make a new friend. You can't know a person's true spirit until you listen to it.

Sally Stopper

From the author:

This book was written for you. It's a story of hope. No matter how far down you have gone, or somebody you know has, change is possible. It is not a guide to recovery, just my experiences that might shine a light on darkness in someone's life.

I would like to say thank you to all those that God sent to me. Without the love he gave you, I would not be here today. Also thank you to my family for all your prayers and hanging in there with me through all those nights and days when you just didn't know what to do. I am also grateful for all the people who encouraged me while writing this book.

When the student is ready, the teacher will appear. Thank you Sally, for the inspiration, and for believing in me. I know none of this would have been possible without you.

Patrick J. Doty

Contents

Less Than Perfect

Introduction

Less Than Perfect

I was sleeping, and awoke to my father standing in the doorway.

I sit up.

"Dad, what are you doing here?"

He replied, "Pat, the man upstairs let me come down and talk to you."

I said, "Dad, you are looking real good. Heaven must agree with you."

He smiled.

It took many years after my Father's death to see him smile at me in my heart the way I saw it that night in the dream.

You see, I lived a life that was, to say the least, Less Than Perfect. We all feel this way at one time or another. No big deal, right? Well, not in my case. See, I had a soul sickness. It was like a cancer eating at my insides, and it affected every part of my life, along with everybody that was a part of it.

Alcoholism and Drug Addiction: I was born with a personality ripe for the picking. Many are not. Some cross a line into it. For me, it was just a matter of taking that first drink, and the wheels were set in

7

motion.

I lived a young life of failure and destruction, which created a lot of feelings of low self-worth and a great deal of guilt that almost killed me by my own doing.

I welcome you to read my story and experience what it means to hang in there one more day. To wake up to a whole new life with a whole new beginning. And when you get there, open your eyes to those who have not made it through yet and help as many as you can.

1

Family

My family is Irish Catholic. That was the recipe for the way we functioned—very traditional with religion, and very religious about being Irish. We did all the things that the Church expected from us, and perpetuated the Irish traditions of drinking and fighting.

Dad comes first. The disciplinarian of the family. Having five kids, four of them very active boys, he needed to be a real stern man. Anytime my mom said, "Your father is on his way home," we straightened right up. Whatever he said goes, with no questions asked.

He was a sales engineer for a company that dealt with electrical switches for elevators. He was up at 5 a.m. every morning—a diabetic, he needed his time alone to eat right and take his shot of insulin. He would usually be gone before everybody else got going.

Dad had a quiet strength about him and was a perfectionist in everything he did. He possessed a good sense of humor; however, when serious, there was no playing around. He showed little emotion, though when he looked at you, you knew he had your best interests in mind.

9

Then there's my Mom. A bit crazy, so I thought. She had the responsibility of every little detail in the lives of five kids. For us boys, Mom was a bit of a pushover. We knew just how to get what we wanted. She always said my father was too tough on us and didn't give us enough attention. She had a soft spot for us, and we took full advantage of it. On the other hand, my sister got away with nothing. Mom was very strict with her, and she was given a lot of responsibilities.

Mom started a daycare business in our home, always wanting to be more than a stay-at-home mom. After a short time she opened a daycare in Keansburg and then another in Matawan. These centers were quite successful and ended up, down the road, supporting our whole family.

The oldest of us kids, and the only girl, is Ellen. Quiet in nature, with a very sweet personality, she was Daddy's little girl. Never in any type of trouble, she was a high achiever in school. I have to say, she stood more in the background of our family dynamics and covered up and cleaned up the trouble and messes us boys got into.

Tim, five years older than me, was always trying to steer us in the right direction. He walked with a lot of pride and tried to be the best at whatever he did. He had the same expectations for the rest of us, and was disappointed when we did not follow his lead. Tim had very firm convictions on the way things should be. He possessed the perfectionism side of my dad; he was not, however, quiet about it. Though he never really understood the rest of us, his intentions were pure.

Then there was Hal, who was two and a half years older than me. Hal and I fought a lot. He had the older-brother syndrome same as Timmy, but, being closer in age, I battled him more. Also, with age in mind, we were a lot closer friends. Outside the house, he always had my back. He tried to talk sense to me. He was firm about his ways, but had a deeper understanding of me than anybody in my family.

I was next in line, the one that would be called the black sheep of the family. Where there was trouble, there was Pat. Loved to antagonize and play jokes on people. Never backed down from anybody or anything. If I was told not to do something, I did it. I know that's a broad statement, but for me, it was a principle I lived by. Having such a strong personality and a nature for trouble, I spent a lot of my younger years going to counseling, with everybody trying to figure me out.

I always wanted to make my dad proud of me, trying hard at whatever I did, excelling in most sports. When doing chores around the house, it was with the approval of my father in mind. Good grades in school, but always in trouble. It wasn't that trouble always seemed to find me, more like I was trying to

11

find it. If it was attention I was seeking, I sure got it.

Last in line was little brother Danny. He hung around me a lot. We were closest in age, just two years apart. He was at the bottom of the totem pole in our family, and I can only imagine the scary place that must have been, especially having me closest to him. He learned to laugh everything off. Danny has a big heart and always sticks up for the underdog. He probably possesses the deepest understanding of the whole family.

On a scale of 1 to 10, I rate my family at a 4; 1 being really dysfunctional, 10 being really healthy for growth. They would probably come in at a 6; however, I am a member of the family, and I easily knock it down 2 points.

My dad liked his beer and my mom liked to cause havoc over his drinking. To this day, I don't know which was worse: his drinking, or her insanity over it. When Dad drank, he was happy and jolly. When he wasn't drinking, he was unpredictable and strict. Him drunk...you could get double and triple allowances. Go to the bar with him...and have a great time. When sober, he would praise you for your work, then in a second, turn on you and pop you one for making a joke.

Dad constantly battled diabetes. For that reason, my mom always hated that he drank...she would say.

But I think she just liked drama. She blamed him for everything that ever went wrong. They fought all the time, and when I say all the time, I mean *all the time*.

There were nights that I lay at my bedroom door, trembling in fear that they were going to kill each other.

One night in particular, Dad had come home drunk. We kids were all in bed. Mom started screaming at him like she always did, and he was laughing at her, calling her crazy. This woke us all up, as it normally did. Mom had lost it. She was throwing things all over. She went to the dishes in the cupboard and started smashing them in the corner of the kitchen. Dad got all of us kids out of bed and lined us up to watch our crazy mother. That night, my mom left for a while. I lay in bed crying all night, thinking Mom was gone for good. I really thought my mom was crazy and we weren't going to have her anymore. She returned home about a week later.

This kind of thing was not an isolated incident for my parents. It was repetitive in many ways. There were many sleepless nights. The same was true for me and my brothers: We fought constantly. I learned to "hit first, ask questions later" at a very young age.

That was the dark side of my family. They also had a lot of good qualities. My mom was always trying to do what she thought best for us kids, making sure our needs were met and dealing with all the troubles that come with that. My dad worked hard and gave us the best. We had all we ever needed. Between them both, we knew nothing of poverty. Dad spent time with us on weekends, playing baseball, basketball, whatever sport we were into at the time.

2

The Move to Belford

I was eight years old when we moved from Northboro, Massachusetts, to Belford, New Jersey, in September 1967.

Belford was a quiet residential section of Middletown Township. The center of town was an old trolley stop, Campbell's Junction, home to a bakery, variety store, butcher shop, deli, and liquor store/bar.

My mother, God bless her soul, is 82 years old. She suffers from middle to late stages of Alzheimer's disease. She is always saying to me, "I should have never moved you guys to Belford." I always reply, "Mom, Belford was not a bad influence on me. I was the bad influence on Belford."

My first memory of that was the moving truck in front of our new home. I was helping move things into the house. Butchy Bair, one of the kids in the neighborhood, came over to check everything out. He wanted to see what was going on and who was moving in. We became best friends from that day on. Later that day, Jimmy Stromberg came along, and we bonded from the start. Jimmy was very outgoing and a comedian, to say the least. Butchy was the opposite. He was quiet in his way. Both were very compatible with me.

I was in third grade, Mrs. Rice's class, in Bayview School. I don't have very many memories of school. I think it's because I absolutely hated it! One thing I do remember was Cheryl, Butchy's sister. She sat behind me and was always trying to get my attention. She would tap me on my shoulders and smile while holding her pigtails in the air.

Cheryl became one of my best friends for years to follow, along with her whole family. Her mom and mine were best friends, and we did a lot together as families. The neighborhood began to grow as we all came together and became friends, with my little brother Danny always tagging along. There was Debbie Stromberg, also in the same grade as me, Jackie Stromberg, a year older, and Terri and Tommy Stromberg, all brothers and sisters of Jimmy's. There were 14 kids in their family.

As time went on, my older brothers Timmy and Hal became friends with Billy and Tommy Evans, and this is how I met Robbie. He was my age. At that point, our neighborhood grew again, adding the Evans and their friends Jeanette and Claudia Wilson and Linda and Debbie Boggart. There were also Jim and Jeff Urbine who lived across the street. I think we fought more than we played together, but nonetheless, we had some really good times. We rode our bikes, played baseball and football, and at one time we all had unicycles and rode them everywhere. We played manhunt till the sun went down.

One time we were playing manhunt in the crow weeds behind our house, near the creek. Danny, my little brother, was looking for us, to no avail. He set the crow weeds on fire to try and get us out. There were fire trucks from both sides of the creek fighting that one. We had our fun times.

Got a little older and played spin the bottle, seven minutes in heaven... kissing games. Kinda dated one another, you know, as kids do, real innocent. I remember Jackie teaching us all how to French kiss. The neighborhood was a real good place.

Less Than Perfect

3

Early Rage

They say there are two sides to every story. That's the way I look at my life. I have shown you that I made a lot of friends and we had a lot of fun right from the start. On the other side, I had a turmoil that ran in me constantly and it needed to be satisfied!

I'll give you an example of the temper and rage that churned in me. I was in third grade, walking home from school. Three kids were following me. I had the sense that they were up to no good and I was about to get jumped. Sure enough, they started throwing rocks at me, calling me names. Well, I wasn't somebody that backed down from anything. I didn't care how many they were—nobody could kick my ass worse than my brothers could. So I turned around and started walking towards them. I spotted an iron rod on the side of the road, bent down and picked it up without them noticing. As I caught up to them, they thought they were going to have their way with me. I began whacking them in their sides, on their backs, whacking their legs, just went mad. I chased them right into their house. Their mother came out, screaming at me, me screaming at her. I took the iron rod and threw it right through their picture window. That was my first encounter with the law.

I went home, and the police came shortly after. No charges were ever brought up on me; however, my parents had to pay for the broken window, and I had to work it off around the house. Even at that age, I feared nobody but my father.

4

Beer and Smoking

When I was in fourth grade, Joey, a friend from school, and I started smoking. We didn't do it because of peer pressure; we did it to get away with it. Soon after that, I started stealing beer from my father. I would take a bottle down to the creek behind our house and drink it. It made me feel whole and confident. I always had an uncomfortable fear in me, and the beer took it away. I clearly remember telling myself "I am going to do this every day." So I did.

As I got older—I mean a lot older, like 12 years old—I was drinking almost every day. Nobody knew about it, not even my friends. I was smoking all the time, too. I think I was the first one in our school to get suspended for smoking in the bathroom in sixth grade. My older brothers were starting to party a lot, and I fit right in, tagging along with them and their friends on weekends.

The next year, in seventh grade, I started smoking pot. I began by smoking a joint at the bus stop before school with a few people. Eventually, I turned my friends on to it. Then, in no time, we were all doing it regularly.

So we are all drinking, smoking pot, still doing some

21

kid things, but now, doing them high—and always looking to get high. Pop Warner football went by the wayside. I got kicked off for not showing up for practice. Baseball, I had lost interest in. I still liked wrestling, and I did that for a few more years. In the neighborhood, we played a lot of sports and did different things, but getting high was priority.

5

Police a Second Time

My second encounter with the Middletown police came on a Sunday morning. Now, I don't remember if we had been out drinking all night or were just skipping church, but what I do know is I was 13 and I was with Tommy Stromberg. We drank a bottle of vodka and decided we were going to hitchhike to Chips Folly in South Jersey. This is where our friend Butchy and his family were on vacation. We thought it would be fun to join them. We were hitchhiking down Cherry Tree Farm Road, and didn't even come close to making it out of town, when a police car pulled over. Tommy told me to let him do the talking. He was a couple of years older than me, and his brother-in-law was a police officer. Well, that had turned out okay, because they just took us home to sleep it off—so they thought. We both went in one door of our houses and out the other. We met right back up and began our journey again.

We didn't make it too far. This time we got to Campbell's Junction, which was only five blocks away. We were sitting on the wall behind Tony's delicatessen when two cop cars pulled up. I don't think we were in any shape to go much further, even if the cops hadn't shown up. Tommy, again, was the one to do the talking, while I lay drunk on the back of the cop car. Well, for some reason the cop didn't like

23

that. It was a blur to me. Whether I said something to provoke him, which would be the best explanation, because that would have been what I was like, I don't remember. The next thing I know, one of the cops was holding my hands down on the trunk, the other was beating them with the cuffs. I was handcuffed and thrown in the back of the car. What happened to Tommy....I don't know. I don't remember him again on this day.

As we were riding to the station, I was running my mouth, telling the cop what a piece of shit he was, threatening him and probably his family too, knowing me. He was smashing me in the face as we were driving. I couldn't sit back because of the handcuffs, but I didn't care.... I could take a beating, and it just made me stronger and crazier. We got to the station. As we were getting out of the car, he threw me on the ground. I had no shirt on and my hands were cuffed behind my back, so I landed on my chest and face, on the pavement. Ripped me pretty good, but still I was feeling no pain.

We get in the station, and I sweet-talked him into taking the cuffs off. I was like that. I could turn on a dime from a madman to sweet-as-pie to get what I wanted. He took them off, and I busted him right between the eyes. I busted his nose and his glasses. Man, there were cops beating the living hell out of me, like I wasn't already beat to shit. Needless to say there was a trip to the hospital for me after that. They had ripped both shoulder blade muscles in my back, my face was beat to hell, my hands and chest were just a bloody mess, and I had one mad dad. Mad at the Middletown cops.

You just don't know the effect this had on me at that age. My dad was close to the same age I am now, and I can only imagine how he felt at that time. I have children, and I don't know what I would have done. That day put a hatred in me for authority, and a self-loathing as a son that you cannot comprehend unless you've lived it.

My only goal in life at this time, in my heart of hearts, was to make my dad proud of me, and in my mind, I was not even close. There were always two things going on in me and neither of them came close to one another. Which one was going to win out? Well, for now, you can see which Pat was ahead in this battle.

I was charged with assault and battery on a police officer, and my dad pressed charges against the cop who arrested me. Not only was this a big change in me, but it changed my dad, too. He had grown up to respect the police—that day changed his view of them, and I know he second-guessed himself as a father. The charges were dropped down to drunk and disorderly in a plea bargain to drop the charges against the police officer. I was given probation for a year.

6

Change for My Parents, and Me

At this time, my parents began making a lot of changes for themselves in a very positive way, whereas I began my changes in the totally opposite direction. My mom had started going to Al-Anon, battling with my dad more about his drinking, but in a healthier way. My dad was getting sicker all the time with his diabetes, and was in and out of the hospital regularly. He was becoming weaker in body, and you could tell he was questioning himself as a man, husband, and father. He sobered up, but his illness kicked his ass--he was a very proud man, and it killed him to show any weakness. He was losing control of his health, and I felt he knew he was losing control of me. I knew that, but could not help it. I secretly had a respect and love for my father that I was unable to express, but I wasn't able to live or function by his wishes.

That last incident with the police was all over the neighborhood. The kids were bragging about me, and I loved it. I liked being a bad boy. I got a lot of good feeling from it, and I decided that it was more of who I was than the person I was trying to be for my father. Feeling good was what I was going to go with, and that was that!

Anything that I had ever wanted to do or be that was good got sunk, real deep down inside me. Bad had become good. Kids followed me. I was fun, talked about, became the life of the party. Who would want anything different?

So going into eighth grade, my focus on things was much different. Everything I had going on in seventh started to become a way of life. Skipping school regularly. Partying with my older brothers' friends during school hours. They could skip school and get away with it because they were in high school; me, I got caught all the time, but didn't care.

I got a lot of detention, if I even decided to go to school. I was learning to do whatever I wanted and had no respect for anybody. If school gave me a hard time I just would not go. If home gave me a hard time I just would not go home. It was that simple. The last day of eighth grade, we got out at 10 a.m. As we were getting on the bus, I threw a pack of firecrackers under a teacher's feet. I did not get to go home with everybody that day. Mom came and got me. I was suspended for the first ten days of ninth grade, which didn't matter to me. I was just skating through anyway.

In ninth grade I was getting high all the time, drunk on weekends and sometimes during the week. By this time I was dabbling in heavier drugs: acid, angel dust, THC, and mescaline. I was learning how to

27

balance my drinking with my drug use so I wouldn't get into fights so much and avoid my constant interaction with the law. I had been arrested a few more times. Pretty much the same thing I wrote about earlier, except at this point I did the hitting first. Life was just one big party, and I couldn't see it any other way.

7

Kicked Out of School

The following year meant some more changes for me. (Well, to normal people they would be. To me, it was just me.) I was 15 going on 16, loving sex, drugs, and rock and roll and getting into fights, still small, but strong. I was already on probation till I was 18. I had to go to counseling and group therapy. All that, just to keep from being put away. My parents always had an attorney just for me and my interactions with the law.

A couple of us were at the high school this day--the one I was supposed to be attending. We were in the stairway, tripping our asses off. I had about 80 hits of mescaline in my pocket. I am peaking on this stuff and I've got to pee. I keep going to the door, looking down the hall to see if the coast is clear to go to the bathroom. Finally I decide to go, and walk out into the hall toward the bathroom across from the office, hoping nobody comes out. The hallway is closing in on me. I don't know what the hell I'm doing. The principal comes out of the office and walks toward me.

At this time I am thinking, "He doesn't know me." This was a new school for me. It's my first year in high school, and I never went to school for him to know me. Man, this was something. I am tripping like

29

crazy. He walks right up to me and says: "Mr. Doty, I have been wanting to catch up with you for some time. Follow me." So I did. Went into the office, had a seat, and sat there for about an hour. While I sat there, kids were coming in and out, and I was selling my mescaline. I think I sold pretty much all of it. He finally calls me in his office and I sit down. He puts this stack of pink slips on his desk, slides them out like a deck of cards (now don't forget, I am peaking on this stuff), looks me dead in the eyes, and says: "What are we going to do about these?" I'm sorry, but I fell to the ground laughing, I could not say anything, I could not control my laughing. I fell to the ground in tears with laughter. I bet the whole school could hear him screaming at me. He literally chased me right out the front doors and told me he didn't want me ever to step foot on that school's property again. My thoughts were, "Well, how the hell am I going to sell my drugs?"

I'd like to say this affected me in some way, but it didn't. It pretty much was normal life, just a story. A week later, on my 16th birthday, something happened to me that made me start to second-guess my life.

8

16th Birthday

Party at the Strombergs' house. Nothing new, just what we did all the time. Partying, getting drunk, girls, smoking pot and so on. This night, I got into a fight with Tommy Evans. He was a lot bigger than me, and stronger. My chances of beating him were slim to none. Sixteen, I was not fully grown yet. Tommy was two years older, and he clearly had the advantage. Kicking my ass was little problem for him. I was so drunk and he had every advantage. I truly turned out to be the big loser in this one. Maybe. Depends on how you look at it.

Typical of me, Tommy was kicking my ass all over the place and I was going to get him, no matter what. After taking my beating, I left the party. I walked home--only right around the corner--and went into my house. It was late... 2 a.m., maybe. My brother Tim was sleeping, and I snuck into his room to steal his van keys. Steal them I did. I was going to run Tommy over...that was my plan. It was February and the streets were covered in packed snow. I pulled out, drove down the road, stopped in front of Strombergs', screaming at Tommy, telling him what I was going to do, daring him to come out. I think I was becoming a real pain in the ass to him by now. I took off around the block, didn't know what the hell I was doing. I came barreling down the road. I looked

31

at the speedometer, and I was going 90 miles an hour. Right then I knew I was in trouble. The streets were solid ice and snow. I was on a straightaway, but I knew a bend was coming up. I tried slowing down, hitting the brakes, but that was not going to work. At that moment, I blacked out. I don't mean passed out--my eyes just blackened. I could not see a thing. I hit a telephone pole at 90 miles an hour, dead in the middle of the front end of the van.

I remember being trapped, kinda standing against the door of the driver's side. The window was open, and Jimmy Stromberg was standing there telling me, "Come on, Pat, the cops are going to come." The engine in the van had been pushed back to the seat behind me, yet I didn't have a scratch on me. I felt that night that I had been saved for some reason.

Well, needless to say the cops caught up with me and I was arrested again. I got a suspended sentence for a year, and ended up having to go to treatment for alcoholism as part of the plea bargain. This was the first time I ever thought maybe all this trouble wasn't worth it. In some ways I was tired of getting in trouble. But that was fleeting.

9

Getting Even for Danny

The next couple of years went on pretty much the same way. Drugs increased. Probation was always trying to straighten me out. I think my probation officer had a big heart for me: It's the only reason I can think of for why he always kept me out of jail. People really liked me. I just didn't like me. I needed the praise and acknowledgment of being bad to be okay. I also think by this time, I was fully addicted to being just blown out of my mind.

When I was 18 I fell in love, totally smitten, with Dee Dee. It was a real fun summer, lots of kids, partying, barrels, bonfires. We were really mastering the party scene. Now there was singing and guitars. Our parties were huge. People came from everywhere.

I tried to change a little at this time. I had gotten three drunken-driving tickets in like a month. Again more trouble. Went to treatment again. I wasn't ready to stop, but wanted to not get in trouble. I had a girlfriend, and really wanted to change for her. It was making me think. I was torn.
I began a battle with the demons of my inner being.

My dad was getting sicker. He didn't work anymore. I was always creating havoc in our home. One night the police busted their way in my house and pushed

33

my dad onto the floor to go through the rooms looking for me. It was for something I did, I was not innocent. But the thing that got me is the humiliation my dad had to experience. I couldn't walk through the Junction without a cop throwing me on a car and searching me. The cops always parked on the side of the road just down the street, watching our house.

Around this time, my older brothers had an altercation with the police at the carwash, kind of a little rumble with them. We'd had situations like this before, but it never panned out well for the police. My dad hired good lawyers and was in our corner, because he had no respect for them any longer.

After that fight at the carwash, something had happened with my little brother, Danny. I am sure we did something to a cop, and were running through the woods. Danny fell, and they caught him. The one cop recognized him as a Doty and smashed him in the back of the head. He had to get 70 stitches.

A few nights later, I was feeling pretty good. I had matured quite a bit in size and strength. My fighting ability made me untouchable to many. I got the bright idea that I was going to call the cops on myself. I was going to get even for my little brother. By this time, I truly believed that I was going to die fighting the Middletown police. I fantasized about it all the time. And sometimes when I got drunk, I think the devil took over my body. Well, he did this night. I was standing outside a friend's house. I took a big rock and threw it through my windshield, and went in her house and called the police. I told them somebody had just broken the windshield of my car. Then I went out to the driveway and waited for them to come, drunk, but feeling really strong and just plain old mad. Here they come, two cop cars pull up. They both walk up to me, and lo and behold, the cop that busted my brother's head open was one of them, and he recognized me. He looks me right in the eyes and says: "What's the problem?" I turned toward my car and said: "The problem is that you busted my little brother's head open" and boom, I smashed him so hard that he went out like a light. I turned and belted the other cop before he knew what was going on. This guy was like 6'6". He dropped to his knees, I grabbed his arm and bent it back and smashed his face into the ground. I then took the cuffs off his belt and handcuffed myself, got into the back of the car, and told him: "Now you can arrest me."

I took a beating, but that was nothing new. They had me handcuffed to the chair in the police station. I remember the big one taking a shot at me. I was laughing at him, telling him: "You hit like a girl. My little brother could hit harder," and making fun of them about how easy they went down. I told the big guy if he was so big, "Why don't you take the cuffs off?" Then I said: "Never mind. I don't want to shame you anymore." I told them they could beat me all they wanted, but if they laid a hand on anyone in my family again, that one day, they would not be getting up off the ground like I let them up tonight. I got tremendous satisfaction from that night, and I think the cops got the message that they were beginning to get in over their heads with me.

In the past, we had harassed them in so many different ways, but now they saw just how crazy I was. After that night they pulled back. I don't know if it was because my dad was always pressing charges or they just had enough of me. They still had a watch on us all the time, but they never touched us again. We had at least a hundred people at our real good parties and probably 20 to 40 at our regular get-togethers on the corner, and they just watched...nothing.

They charged me good that night, and I was of age, so I was facing some time in the state pen if I was found guilty. But again, my parents came through. We had charges against them, and some police had been suspended because of my dad. He made all that disappear to keep me from getting put away. I got a suspended sentence, the charges were dropped down, and I was placed on probation for an extended time. I came out a free man--not really, but free from jail.

And in some sick way, I think my soul had taken some rest.

10

Motorcycle Accident

My rage for the police had subsided. It did not leave, but it was considerably less. I started caring about life. The question here is, was I capable of it?

Sometime that year, my Mom had purchased an old military academy. She had two daycare centers, and merged them both together into this new one. This was an opportunity for me. I started working for her full-time renovating the buildings. I brought on a few of my friends, and we really went to town on the place. It had many buildings to it, so the work was plentiful.

My whole family moved out of Belford and into the main building. I think my parents thought that this would be really good for us, but our roots were already planted. As time went on, I was still partying pretty heavily, but at the same time, trying to be somewhat responsible. My dad was just getting sicker all the time, in and out of hospitals. He was having a lot of convulsions coupled with grand mal seizures. They could not figure it out, so they just said he got epilepsy from years of insulin use. I was trying to balance my alcohol, my drug use, and being a boyfriend and a son. I had never tried this before. I was succeeding to some degree, though others might argue that point.

37

People were always telling me, If you just curb your drinking, you'll be alright. I think at one point in my life that was so, but not now. It was too late. I believe I had cancer of the soul. The demons of my life were just eating me away. I was sneak-drinking and functioning on drugs. Partying with friends, still getting into fights when I really put one on, but hiding a lot of my activities. My soul was in great conflict. Dee Dee would not put up with me, either. I wanted to have a life with her, but there just wasn't anybody home. In me, that is.

I became a water safety instructor and was working with the summer camp at my Mom's school. I gave the kids swimming lessons and taught the teachers life-saving techniques. It was a good, easy job.

One day I was running late for work. I had been out drinking all night. I had gotten a Kz 1000 motorcycle from my brother Hal. At the time, this motorcycle was the fastest one made. I was riding it to work and in a hurry.

Between the speed of this bike and the fact that I was still filled with alcohol, it was a recipe for disaster. Coming down the road at 80 miles an hour, I came up on a slight bend. It was enough not to see the other side of it, but not enough to slow down. As I came around the corner there was a car getting ready to turn across my lane. "Oh, shit, Oh no!" Right at this moment everything went into slow motion for me. This all happened in a split second, but not in my mind. They were turning. I was going to die.

There was absolutely no way I should have survived this accident. Eighty miles an hour, head on? Come on, you just don't walk away from that! With quick reflexes, I put my feet on the seat. How I knew to do that, to this day, amazes me. On impact, I was jetted up and out. I was above the telephone polls, and it felt like I was being carried. I came down into oncoming traffic, bouncing like a basketball. I could see a car coming right for me. I somehow knew that if I put my right arm under me, I would roll to the left out of oncoming traffic, kind of like if a ball hit a rock and bounced off in a different direction. I then jumped to my feet. I remember people coming running over to me saying: "You're in shock, lay down." Me saying: "Leave me alone, I'm fine." My helmet was cracked in the back and looked like a spider web, and I had some pretty bad road rash. Again, like the van accident, there was no way I should have survived. I think the devil was told "no" one more time. I was really beginning to believe there was a purpose for my life. I absolutely knew that there were angels carrying me through that.

11

Leaving Dad

By this time, Dee Dee and I had been going out for at least two years, maybe a little longer. She saw no future with me, and I knew it. Our relationship just started falling apart.

My dad was paralyzed on his right side. He was so stubborn and proud, he learned to write with his left hand. The parties went on, life changed, Dee Dee and I broke up.

My dad was diagnosed with a brain tumor. He went into the hospital and was there for about a month. They had decided to try and operate. I was with my mom when she made the decision to let them. The tumor had been growing for at least six years, they said. All the time, they were looking in the wrong spot.

I was nursing my wounds over being heartbroken, relieved in a way that I could drink like I wanted to, but heartbroken nonetheless. A friend of mine was moving down to Florida, where his family had moved a few years earlier. I had decided to go with him. I took a special trip to the hospital to tell my father I was leaving town.

I walked in the room. My dad was looking at me. He

just laid there in bed, half his body paralyzed. I was scared, because I knew what I was doing was wrong. My dad could not talk anymore. He just looked at me. I said, "Dad, I am leaving for Florida with a few friends. I need to get my life together, and I can't do it here." Dad just looked at me. It felt like he was looking right through me. My eyes started to tear. I knew I would never see him again. I turned and walked out. We both were full of pride, and him seeing any tears in my eyes was the last thing I wanted. I never, ever saw a tear fall from his face.

So off I went, to Florida, on my selfish drunken escapade while dad lay dying in the hospital.

We got down there and I started working right away with my friend Dave, and we stayed at his parents' house. Yes, drunk every night and worked every day. About a week had gone by. We came home from work, and Dave's mother was waiting in the driveway to greet us. I thought it was strange. His step dad was there, too. We got out and walked over to them. I knew. "Pat, your father passed away today." I knew, I knew, but I was floored.

I flew home for his funeral. I was a pallbearer, along with my brothers, and whoever else. It's such a blur. I was 20 years old. I just drowned myself in alcohol. I no longer cared about anything...no more trying to be good...no more trying to be somebody. I just could not face myself.

When my dad died, I felt like there was nothing more for me. So drenched in self-pity. The devil didn't want to be denied. I had terrible nightmares of carrying my father's coffin and the bottom falling out, his body rolling down the driveway hill. The same dream, over and over again. It was how I felt. I had desecrated his life...over and over again.

12

The Dream

Before Dad passed, I had started another addiction—speed. Now back in New Jersey, I was using a needle. I was binge drinking for days at a time, staying mostly at my friend Jeff's house. We drank constantly and used different drugs, but Jeff didn't shoot up like I did. My needle use got real bad. Eventually I chose it over drinking. I was shooting speed for 10 or 11 days straight, no sleep, then crashing for 3 or 4 days...all the time.

The speed was catching up to me. I was watching the people who were shooting speed go down the tubes quickly from it. A lot of my close friends were just staying away from me. But I still had Jeff. I felt like he believed in me. His mom fed me and made sure I was taken care of, and we ran...drinking, partying, girls. We used to go to Atlantic City all the time. We had good fun.

His brother Steven was crazier than I was. We did things that I can't speak of for money and drugs. I got high with Steven... drunk with Jeff... until the needle got the best of me. Then I tried to just drink so I could stay away from it. One morning, me and Chris, another friend, decided we would take off for Florida to get away from drugs.

I was coming off a run of speed, and I was home sleeping it off.

I had a dream...maybe it was real. It was very clear. I was sleeping and awoke to my father standing in the doorway.

I sit up....

"Dad, what are you doing here?"

He replied:

"Pat, the man upstairs let me come down and talk to you."

I said:

"Dad you are looking real good. Heaven must agree with you."

He smiled. He looked like he was about 30 years old...very healthy and strong.

He said:

"Follow me. I have something to show you."

We walked out into the kitchen, and in there were a bunch of people partying, with a barrel of beer in the sink.

He told me:

"Pat, you have to get away from these people and you have to do it fast."

Me:

"Even from the grave you're trying to get me to stop drinking."

Dad:

"No, Pat. Just get away, and get away now. If you do, God has a very special life planned for you. If you don't, you are going to die a very horrible death."

We walked back to my room, and I got in bed. He was standing at the door and started getting old and sick, real skinny like before he died, eyes all bloodshot.

I asked him:

"Dad, what's going on? How come you are getting sick?"

He replied:

"Pat, I am hurting for you. Please get away from these people."

Chris and I split town to get away from drugs. We went to Daytona, where my Uncle Butch lived, a true Irishman. Uncle Butch was always real good to me, the one person in my family that I could relate to. He was always very hard on me, but I understood him. Anyway, Uncle Butch took us in with open arms and was always there for me.

In Daytona, we continued to party a lot; however, we were getting away from the drugs. I had my conflicts with my uncle, but it was family, and I know to this day, God rest his soul, it was all good.

The next year, I kept taking off and going to

different parts of the state, and in a lot of cases, different parts of the country. My uncle's house is where I always returned to get rejuvenated. There were times when I would find myself sleeping in parks, cars, abandoned houses, eating out of dumpsters, stealing food from grocery stores. Just becoming a real-life bum. Sometimes it was like living on skid row. I met up with some people and we drove to Louisiana, then Kentucky, then back to Daytona, fighting, partying, stealing, you name it. I was always getting picked up by the police for vagrancy. I spent many nights in the county jail in Daytona, a few times it was months. Could not stay sober or out of jail...a real low-life.

I have many stories to tell, but the real story was that I was done with it all but didn't know how to stop. I was having different nightmares, bad ones with bad things happening to people because of me. One day, I called my Mom and asked her for a ticket home. She told me that she would give it to me if I went to treatment. I agreed. I flew home.

13

Detox

Mom picked me up at the airport. My hair was down to the middle of my back. I was only 130 pounds and looked like hell. I told Mom that I would go, but I was not doing everything they wanted. She agreed with anything I said, just to get me there. We walked in my house, and my grandmother was there. She looked at me, with tears in her eyes, and slapped me right across the face and told me to get a haircut. Pat, being Pat, split. Didn't go to treatment.

I had to go sow my oats for the first few days. It was Christmas, and there were a lot of parties. I hadn't been home in a while.

For the next week, I ran wild, seeing everybody, drunk the whole time, running with Jeff.

Me and Steven were planning to hold up the Sunoco station in Atlantic Highlands. He had it all planned out, and I was in, didn't matter to me. We were just having a grand old time. Well, New Year's Eve, I was drinking whiskey and passed out. Steven decided to go without me. Maybe he couldn't wake me, I don't know. We had been planning it for days. He ended up taking somebody else, and he got busted. For me, that was a close call. Not for him, though. I knew I should have been there with him, and my time was up. I called Mom and told her I was ready. She came and got me and took me right to detox. It had been a long time since I had been without anything in my system, so this was no joy ride.

I went to detox. Sick, oh, My God, was I sick. In that week in detox, I had something happen to me. I really wanted a better life, to change as a person and all that, but I couldn't shake the hard-ass I was so that I could surrender to their direction for me. I think God kinda did it for me. He said: "The devil ain't getting you, boy. You're mine." And I thought: "This is gonna be some fight."

I was sitting on this little two-seater bench at the end of the hall. I had been in there almost a week. I was feeling better in body than I had been, but my soul was eating away at me. And then it was as if I was wearing a straitjacket that suddenly started to unravel and just disappeared up into the ceiling. What happened was God allowed me to have acceptance for the first time in my life. I was an alcoholic, and it was alright. Boy, what a feeling--you could only know what it was like if it had happened to you. I walked in peace for days. They wanted me to go to treatment, and I was more than happy to oblige them...so off to treatment I went.

Man, I thought I had this licked for the first time in my whole life. I felt like I was going to do right and mean it. I went 30 days, then got out, went back home. I went to AA meetings every day, but something wasn't right. I wanted to "do the deal" as they say in AA, but I wasn't relating to anyone. I still felt different from everybody.

Michael, Jeff and Steven's older brother, was in the program and sober. He was real happy and walked with a peace that I truly admired. He was from Belford and I knew what he was like, so I attached myself to him and asked him to be my sponsor. Boy, was that weird. I humbled myself. It was strange, and I didn't like having to ask him, but that's what you were supposed to do. That was about as much humility as I wanted. He said yes.

I wasn't ready. I could not talk in meetings. I could not share how I felt. I had not felt feelings in many, many years. They were weird to me. I had drowned them in booze and drugs for so long, they were just not there. The only thing I had was the fact that I didn't want to drink. Michael had changed, so why not me?

I went on that way for a few months, and it got bad. I was just miserable and couldn't do anything about it. Michael would look at me and say: "That bad, huh, Pat?" He knew, but couldn't help me. I was trapped. Because of this, I couldn't get anything out of meetings. I would go there in agony and leave the same way. No desire to get drunk or high, but I wanted relief.

I got my 90-days-sober pin. First time I ever did it. I

left that meeting and went and picked up a six-pack...just hurting. I looked at that beer for like an hour. Then finally, I cracked one...I drank it straight down...another, then another. It felt good. I went to Jeff's house. We got drunk for a few days. We were in his truck down at the docks, drinking beer. Michael appeared. He had been out on a fishing boat. He walked up to the truck to say hi. I felt two inches tall. He just looked at me and said: "That's alright, Pat. You'll get it." This man had such a gentle spirit.

Jeff and I had ended up back at his house. We got our hands on some THC. I shot it, he snorted it. I seemed to not be getting relief as we were blasting our minds out. I kept telling Jeff that I couldn't do this anymore. I remember him telling me: "Pat, you are going to make it, because you want it." I got a bright idea. I didn't tell Jeff, but it was my plan. I was going strong with the THC in me and I figured if I bought a bottle of vodka and drank it as fast as I could, it would stop my heart and kill me. I was going to do that. It felt good. So I told Jeff: "Let's go get some vodka," with him not knowing what my plan was. I went into Junction Liquors, picked up a bottle of vodka, and went over to pay for it. There was somebody in front of me, so I had to wait.

I felt a hand grab my shoulder, and it was my brother Hal. He looked at me and said: "What the hell are you doing?"
"Simple. I'm buying a bottle."

"You are done with that," said Hal. "You're going to kill yourself."

Little did he know, that is what I had planned.

"Hal, I have tried to get sober. I can't. I can't do it. This is me. Leave me alone."

Hal was not taking that for an answer.

"Listen, buddy, you can make a scene if you want, but you're coming with me."

I had no fight in me. I was beaten, weak, and at death's doorstep.

"I'm taking you home, and you can sleep this off and go back to that AA of yours."

I told him that it would not work. I would do that with all the best intentions, but I would be right back out drinking.

"I don't want to drink. I *have* to. Hal, if you really want to do right by me, please take me to detox at the hospital."

He agreed. I wouldn't see Jeff again for nine years. I was so messed up and bombed.

14

Back to Detox

They welcomed me back to detox. I felt at home there. That is where I belonged. I sobered, detoxed, as you might have it, but I was dead inside. I didn't even know if I had a soul. I was in such a state of despair. I wish it on nobody. If you ever had any thoughts of what hell was like, I was there.

I prayed, "God take me. Take this life. Close the coffin. I can't take one more step. Please, Lord, another life, some other time. I can't do it." With all my heart I wanted to die. The demons were eating me alive inside, bite after bite, and I couldn't do anything about it.

So there I am in detox. Hell wants me more than ever. I am so close to heaven, and the demons are biting at me hard. A few days go by. I am not feeling any better. I get called into this room and there is a circle of chairs.

I figure this is my fate coming. Now I am going to hear it. Didn't care. I sit. Other people are there. I don't know how many, a few. This was an intervention. First thing they say to me: "How you feeling, Pat?" "What the fuck?" That was my first response...out loud. "Don't tell me you called me in here to ask me how I feel. Take a gun, stick it in my mouth, and blow my brains all over that wall. That's how I feel." This lady, Judy, came over and sat right next to me. She told me: "Don't worry, just hold on." She knew right where I was, and I felt that it was good. They proceeded with their intervention.

"First of all, we are never going to let you come back here again."

My head said:

"Oh, here we go."

"This is what we want you to do."

I had a moment of sanity. How could they think I would do anything? I never did before. I always conned my way out of everything.

They said:

"Pat, this is what we want you to do. You are going to a six-week program down in south Florida. Then you are going to live in a halfway house for six months. Then you are going to live in a sober house until you are two years sober. If you don't do this, we don't ever want to see you again."

My God! Relief finally came into my soul. Those demons just took a heavy hit. I was more than happy. God had listened. He did take my life and gave me a new one. That's how I felt. I can only say "Wow!" It was great news.

So Mom came and got me a few days later. She took me to the airport for the flight to Palm Beach, Florida. On the way, she told me, "Just stay teachable." I understood what she meant.

On the plane ride down, I sat with a bunch of girls going there for spring break. I had fun. Good ride, loved the girls. I get there and a guy named Jim picks me up. He was the husband of Judy, the lady in the intervention. It was like I was family, and I took it all in, like never before.

15

The Beach Comber

When I got to treatment, I was placed on three days blackout. This meant that I was not allowed to leave with the other clients to go to the beach or for walks. No biggie!

There were eight cottages, two people per cottage. The main house had a big room where we broke down for group sessions, set up for meals, and congregated at night, playing cards and just associating with each other. From there you walked into the kitchen. A lady named Penny was the cook. She was sweet, and later on in life, I became real good friends with her and her whole family, another mom for me.

While in treatment, we were given reading and writing assignments. I was teachable, but pretty illiterate. I struggled with these a lot, so they just let me slide on them. They told me to write my life story as best I could while I was there. My spelling was terrible, but my counselor told me I wrote very well. That felt good, because I really did feel like an idiot about writing. When I was called on in meetings, we talked about the things I wrote.

I was receiving a lot of letters from different girls, and they didn't think that was appropriate. They started to believe that I had women issues, along with everything else. I was told to block them out and not respond. No women for a year they said at first, but later it got pushed to two years, as they dug deeper.

I was off blackout and allowed down to the beach. We had a two-hour break for lunch and beach in between group sessions and our teachings on addiction. We went to the beach every day, as it was only a block away. After dinner, we went on long walks on the beach and in the neighborhood. At night we had group meetings, laid-back ones. Sometimes people would come in and speak to us, other times there were movies on addiction. We received chips for the amount of days we were sober—it was cool.

About a week had gone by in my treatment, and I had begun to have an affair with a girl in treatment. She was 30 years old and married, with a child. We had sex every night the rest of the time I was in there. I knew it was wrong. I met her husband on visiting days and did feel bad, but I loved the thrill of it. And there was no way I was going to tell anybody, not because I was afraid of getting in trouble, but because I didn't want her to get in trouble or hurt her family. I kept this a secret for many years. However, when I got out of treatment, I knew sex was just another addiction that I had to confront, and I did.

Four weeks had gone by, and they told me I had to go for an interview for a halfway house. I was a little shocked, because I thought I was there for six weeks. I sat down at my counselor's desk and said, "I'm not ready." She said, "Yes, you are." "No way. You don't know me. I will drink again. I always do." I busted down crying. I don't remember ever doing that before, not even at my dad's funeral. I pleaded for my life: "I can't leave."

This was exactly what I needed if I was to have any hope for recovery. I had not shown any real emotions for many years. It was a sign that there was hope for me. I still doubted myself, but I was willing to do what I was directed to do, and I held on to that for dear life.

16

Palm Trail Lodge

So, off to the halfway house. Nothing like treatment. It was half way into the world, with imposed structure and monitoring of your life. This was good. Palm Trail Lodge was its name, and it was located in Delray Beach, Florida. Close to 30 guys resided there, of all ages and backgrounds.

My roommate's name was Freddy. We were close in age, with similar backgrounds. We had gotten along well, and he had a desire to change too. This was a blessing, because the majority of the guys were only there to stay out of trouble or just get three meals and a cot. We spent a lot of nights staying up talking about recovery.

Jim Nicholson, the man who picked me up at the airport when I went to treatment, set me up with a job at the Gulfstream Golf Course. The course was in between the Intracoastal Waterway and the ocean, just down the street from the Beach Comber. The 18th hole was on the ocean. I was the greens keeper. I mowed the greens every morning, fertilized, and did whatever else was needed. I was a very hard worker, committed to the job 100 percent. This was paradise. Palm trees, ocean, riding around on mowers. Who could want more? My boss, Stanley, was sober for five years. He had the knowledge and understanding of a recovering alcoholic.

After work every day, I road my bike to the Beach Comber and visited. They were my family at the time. A feeling of closeness engulfed the place. Jim Bryant, who owned it, was a very smart man and amazing to be around. He stimulated one's mind and knew people inside and out.

Back at the halfway house there was a different kind of climate. It was smart to pick and choose who to associate with. I was prejudiced against people who were just conning their way through. This was a protective shell, due to the fear that dwelled within me of any possibility of relapse. That fear of getting drunk again somehow showed: It was a negative that worked positively perfectly, a silent anger that kept a lot of people away. Being a newcomer in recovery myself, it was essential to be around the winners, going to AA meetings every night and doing everything that was suggested to me.

Again, 90 days sober. This time, though, I had a level of gratitude that was emotionally healing. It felt like, for the first time in my life, I was becoming what I had wanted to be all my life. In the big book of Alcoholics Anonymous, there are promises, and one of them is: "Things beyond your fondest dream will come into your life." To me, sleeping in the same bed every night and having three meals a day, clean clothes, a shower, and a job to go to every day was beyond my fondest dreams.

Even with the best of dreams, the weather has a
tendency to change. A storm was brewing.

I spoke of a girl I had had an affair with in treatment.
She had left treatment a few days earlier than I did.
We parted with the understanding that we could not
continue what we were doing after she left. I really
wanted to give recovery my all. However, it was
obvious her feelings went much deeper. She was
calling for me all the time, also stopping by looking
for me. After a period of avoiding her, she finally
went away.

Ron was the director there, and he confronted me
on it. You could say this was my first real test of
whether or not I was going to change my old ways
and habits. My grade on this one? Probably 50%. I
lied about it, told him she was just infatuated with me
and I could not get rid of her, which was a half-truth.
Under normal circumstances, this would be nobody's
business but my own. But, rigorous honesty was my
only hope, and keeping secrets from the people who
were helping me was going in the wrong direction.
This was a feeling of failure that hung with me for a
while.

After completing three months in the halfway house,
I was told it was time for me to move on. I went to
live with Jimmy and Judy Nicholson for the next year
and a half, riding my bike everywhere, working on

the golf course, and following the directions of my counselors. Life was simple and really good. This was the treatment I needed to have half a chance for recovery.

I can describe this time of my life in two words: Alcoholics Anonymous. That's all this period was about, getting myself planted in the program and adopting that way of life. I had grown considerably as a person, and became very active in the program. My life was filled with good friends and people of all types.

You could be sitting in a meeting and on one side of you would be a homeless person who had lost everything, his family, self-respect, and means of support. On the other side would be one of the most prominent people in America, extremely wealthy, with all the backing of his family, and associates of his business and life rooting for him. The minute they walked into the rooms of AA, there was absolutely no difference between the two. Both were there for the same reason. This sickness had no respect of person.

Back in those early days, I worked the 12 steps with my sponsor. Every week we met and read from the books of AA. We talked about ourselves and saw things from a recovering aspect. It was a time of great personal change. I had a lot of social insecurities. My personality was a little withdrawn. However, in time it bloomed, letting down my defense mechanisms, staying active, and living day to day with purpose.

A group of us started an AA clubhouse in Delray Beach, where you could congregate in your free time, play video games, shoot pool, play Ping Pong or cards, and just have a place to go, like a positive replacement for the bar scene. We had dances there on weekends and AA meetings all the time. We called it The Crossroads Club, and it's still operating, 30 years later, playing the same role as it did for us in the lives of many today.

Jimmy and Judy were great to me. They treated me as one of their own. For the first time, I was living in a calm family atmosphere, talking about everything that was going on in my life. It was real easy for me to tell Judy that I was feeling really stupid and didn't think the girls liked me, or even the exact opposite of that, and she had a way of balancing me out that was very gentle and loving. Jimmy had no problem telling me, "You're screwing up. If you keep doing that, there's a drink right around the corner." Or the opposite: "You're doing great. Keep up the good work." I respected what he said. Jeff, Judy's son, was like a little brother to me. It felt good being a positive example to him. This might sound funny, since I was 23 or 24 years old and just learning these things about family myself, but that was the reality of my life, and I welcomed the love.

17

Moving Out

Now two years sober, it was time to move on and get a place of my own. I moved into an apartment and received a letter stating that I was no longer on probation. With help from my counselors, I got my driver's license back. It had been taken by the judge for an indefinite time. I traded in my 10-speed bicycle for a van. I was Stanley's assistant on the golf course. He was the top boss and I was number two. Things had become very special in my life, like my father had said. So I thought.

Out of the watchful eyes of others, demons of my past were waiting around every corner.

Dating began right away. This was Southern Florida, and women were everywhere. Me, 25 years old. First there was the bank teller. She was a real sweet girl, tiny and extremely cute. She was a normal person, and I was anything but normal. Second was a very rich, beautiful girl. She was more my match, but I was always very uncomfortable about the wealth that surrounded her. Then there was a third girl, who more or less just stopped by some nights to enjoy my company. I wasted no time getting in over my head.

I was screwing up at work by oversleeping and coming in late. After doing this a few times, I wouldn't even go in after oversleeping. One time I laid in bed for three days, just gripped with depression. It was so bad I fantasized about having two guns and putting them on each temple and blowing my brains out. Two years of hard work on the golf course was going right down the tubes, and my sobriety was not far behind.

When I went to AA meetings and shared what was going on, people told me to set more alarms or go to bed earlier. I felt like I was being scolded. My self-worth was bottoming out. In my head, I really was just a worthless piece of crap, until one night when I was speaking at a meeting and sharing my life story. While helping others with my story, I received exactly what I needed: being reminded of the hell of my past and that I am now sober. In detox, I had asked God to take this life; somehow I had taken it back. Simple as that. All I needed was to know I did not drink and to allow God to be in control of my life.

Later that week, I met with Ron, my AA sponsor. He had been my counselor in Palm Trail Lodge. A sponsor is someone who guides you through the 12 steps of Alcoholics Anonymous, someone to confide in, not someone to tell you what to do. Just a person you trust to help you see the truth.

Talking to Ron, it was clear to me that my self-worth was still too low to be dating these girls. I was very uncomfortable about the way I was going about it and the way I seemed to be backsliding with work. I really didn't want to be that type of a person. It just didn't feel right. I wanted to live by a higher standard.

My boss, Stanley, was not very pleased with me. He had decided that I was being very careless about work. He said I didn't care about my job anymore, so he fired me. That was a blow, because I thought if I was honest with him, he would understand. Not many alcoholics recover, and Stanley had said to me: "I'm surprised you are sober." I think that he thought since I was on my own and screwing up, he didn't want any part of it. God works in mysterious ways, though. Right around the corner was a much better opportunity for me.

18

Making a Go of It

I started a painting business. It was good in the beginning, but had a lot of ups and downs. Not being much of a self-motivator and prone to spots of depression, I wasn't good at handling the downtimes.

My friend Billy had started a roofing crew for tile roofs. He offered me a job with him, and I accepted. A few weeks into it, he asked me to be his business partner. He, too, was newly in recovery, and having somebody partner with him eliminated some of his fear. Again, I accepted.

We started out with five guys and tapped into a lot of work right away. We were thinking if we could make about $500 a week, we would be happy. That was not even close to what was in store for us. Almost overnight we had grown to 10 guys, then 15, then 20. We were making more money than either one of us had ever imagined. Our lives changed. New trucks, new equipment. I went from a beat-up van that maybe cost $100 to driving a brand-new pickup truck. Stepped up from my little apartment and moved into a two-bedroom house. Nothing fancy, but for me, it was a mansion on the hill.

One morning, I received a call from Zowie, a friend

of mine from Belford. He was in trouble, hitchhiking down to find me, hoping his life could be better. When he got to me, he was a mess. He was living the life of a drug addict and alcoholic. So, we got him sobered up and off drugs, he went to AA meetings, lived with me, and worked for me. It felt good to be helping him, thinking God was beginning to use me to help friends from my past.

About that same time, I started dating my first wife, Jolene. She was also in AA and living sober. It wasn't very long before we moved in together. Having a new girlfriend, it seemed appropriate to have a nicer home, a little more private. I was quickly moving up in the world of finances.

Shortly after moving in together, Jolene had some legal issues she had to deal with. Before going into the AA program, she was driving drunk and hit somebody head on and killed them. This was a tragic thing for everyone involved. Being convicted of vehicular manslaughter, she had to go to jail for three months and then was placed on probation for ten years.

Once out of jail, she told me she wanted to have a baby. Becoming a father sounded really good, so I was game. We got married, and Zowie was my best man. We had a ceremony on the beach, real small, just a few people from the program. Jim Bryant's son Joe married us. He was a justice of the peace. So, off we go getting pregnant.

Around this time, Steven came down from Jersey wanting help to get sober. Just like Zowie, I took him in and gave him work. He went to meetings every day, cleaned up well. Steven was a real good man sober. We became very close friends. He ended up moving in with another guy in the program, then met a girl and married her. Zowie also eventually married his girlfriend. Butchy ended up moving there too. He had met his wife in Daytona. I found them a home right around the block from where we were living. By this time, I had a lot of old Belford friends moving to the area. Butchy came to work for me. He did not get sober right away, but after watching the rest of us for a couple of years, he also became sober and a member of AA. Life was really good, a lot of friends, starting my own family, and being successful in the world.

One time Steven and I were out snorkeling on Boynton Beach reefs. It was a stormy day. There was a nor'easter coming in. The waves were pretty big. The water was really rough. But we thought we were rougher. We went out to the second reef, which was pretty far out. A real rough wave came and pulled us out past the second reef. When the water calmed, there was a school of sharks all around us. I had never seen so many sharks before. I lifted my head up out of the water. Steven did too. At the same time, we looked at each other with a kinda "oh, shit" look.

We swam fast back to shore. We were so far out that by the time we got to shore we were exhausted. We laid on the beach just cracking up at each other about how scared we were. It was a blast. Two tough guys just had the living shit scared out of them!

19

It's a Boy!

All things going according to plan, Jolene was pregnant. I was working down in Fort Lauderdale when her water broke. It was about 45 minutes away from Boynton Beach, where we lived and the hospital was. I hardly remember the drive to the hospital; I think I was just in a daze. When I got there, Jolene was already hooked up to the machine that monitored the baby's heartbeat. Her contractions were real close, and she was in labor.

The doctor and nurses were in the room with us. The baby's heartbeat dropped way down, and I could tell something wasn't right by the way everybody was acting. They told me that the cord was wrapped around the baby's neck and they had to rush Jolene into surgery right away, that my wife's and baby's lives were in danger.

One minute we are having a baby, and in a split second, I'm standing in the room by myself, not knowing what the hell is going on. Pacing like crazy. My emotions were just churning uncontrollably. I remember banging the back of my head on the block wall. Finally the doctor came out and asked, "Do you want to see your new baby boy?" Wow!!! What a relief. I followed the doctor into the room where they were cleaning him up. He handed me our baby, saying: "Don't worry, you won't hurt him." I held him, knowing that everything I was, was for him. The most amazing feeling that there is. Nothing matches that moment. To me, he looked just like my dad. He would have been proud.

After three days, we went home with our newborn baby boy, Patrick.

Life was just getting better and better for us all the time. I was a committed husband and father. Worked hard long hours. Went to meetings. Helped other alcoholics. Truly could not have asked for anything more out of life. I had become everything I ever wanted to be.

Jolene and I decided to move into a bigger home. I was trading houses like I was trading in cars and trucks at that time. I felt as long as I worked hard, I could do whatever I wanted. We moved into a 3,000-square-foot home in Delray Beach, with a two-car garage and beautiful landscaping. I bought Jolene a black Firebird, and we had two brand-new pickup trucks—one basically just sat, and the other I drove all the time. I eventually gave that one to Butchy to use. He was my foreman at the time.

We bought a piece of property in Boynton and were having a new house built. At the time, South Florida was the third-fastest-growing area in America. It was a time of recession for most, but not us. If I worked three days on landing a job and got it, that one job was like 500 homes. That's what we did. One sale was good enough for six months to a year of work. There was so much work that Billy and I split the business in two. Now I had at least 30 guys working for me.

What do you think? Dad was right? God has a special life for me? Well...this was NOT the special life that Dad was talking about.

20

Jolene Gets a Phone Call

Approximately a year and a half goes by. Things seemed pretty stable on the surface. One day, Jolene gets a phone call from a girl she went through treatment with. They made plans to get together and go to a meeting. (This is what I'm told, anyway.) I thought nothing of it. Well, that night she didn't come home. I was up all night worried. I even called the police and had them looking for her. My emotions were frazzled. The next morning, she came strolling in about 8 a.m., drunk.

Anytime somebody stayed at my house, "No Drinking" was a must. I helped a lot of guys get sober, and if they drank, they were out. Well, I handled this no differently. That day, I made arrangements for her to go to the Beach Comber. She didn't go willingly. I told her she could not stay in our house, and if she didn't go, I was calling her probation officer. So she went.

To me this was a huge threat to my life. I had never thought something like this was going to happen, even though that's what alcoholics do: They get drunk. And I married one. I talked to people at meetings and got a little understanding for her. But still, never thought to myself "It could have been me that got drunk."

While she was in treatment, one of the counselors took me aside to talk. She told me the reality of the situation was that some people just don't make it. She didn't think Jolene was going to, and said: "You'd better prepare yourself for that."

With my wife in treatment, some friends were taking care of Patrick during the day so I could work. It was a lonely time. This was something I wasn't used to. I was totally powerless over what she did and how she affected us.

When Jolene got out of treatment, I wasn't ready for her to come home, and I didn't think she was either. She had made arrangements to live with some people who were sober to try and stay sober, but it was not working. She started drinking again.

One day I came home and Jolene was sitting at the kitchen table with Tom and Julie, a couple who were friends of ours. She had asked them to come with her to talk to me. She told me she was sorry and wanted to come back home, promising to stay sober. I was fine with that. When we got married, it was till death do we part. To me, drinking was death. I still maintained a strong sense of prejudice against drinking. I really was a committed husband, so her coming back, sober, was okay with me. If life could get back on track, this was good news.

As we were talking, all four of us, I was still not feeling very comfortable about this meeting. Then

Tom says: "There's more. Go ahead, Jolene. Tell him." She proceeded to tell me she was pregnant and the baby was not mine. My heart dropped. She pleaded with me to forgive her, but I just shut down. That was it. I could not come back from that.

I guess Tom and Julie were hoping I understood or something, but it wasn't in me. It felt like she had stolen all my dreams of having a family. Well, from there, we were done. She got an abortion and moved to a lot of different places. She just went straight downhill.

My life changed. It was Patrick and me from there on in. She came and visited him once in awhile. When she left, he would scream and cry. He just didn't understand, and you could see that in his face. It was heartbreaking. Her visits got fewer and fewer. My mom came and stayed for a little while, then my sister. They just wanted to help me with Patrick. Finally I got a nanny to move in and take care of him and the house.

The whole situation made me very angry. For a long time I judged her hard for this. I knew in my head that she was Patrick's mother, but in my heart, I didn't believe that at all. He was my son and mine only, and I treated her that way. She didn't put up much of a fight with me. I just did what I thought was best for him. Every once in awhile she would think she wanted to be a mother, but her actions never showed it. I remained very protective of him.

I stuffed my anger deep and it came out as depression, and at times, self-pity. I didn't have gratitude in my life any longer, and blamed God for this. Where's my special life?

21

Lost

Working long hours, going to meetings, dating different girls. I just kind of shut down on things I thought were important at one time, and started over in a way.

One day, somebody came to me with an opportunity to start a cultured-marble business. It was a big thing then. Cultured marble was used in almost all the new homes. It was a no brainer. With the contacts I had, I could sell this stuff to all the developers. With the huge hit taken to my self esteem and family dreams blown apart, I thought this was my cure-all. In my insanity, I started a new business venture. A new energy. A new lease on life.

My house in Boynton was under litigation because the developers that were building it went bankrupt. I had been trying to get my money back. The bank that was backing the development took everything over, and I had a lawyer working on it for me. He called me and asked if I wanted them to finish the house or get my money back. I chose the money, because the house was with Jolene, and I didn't want any part of it. I took that money and made my first purchase of equipment, molds, and materials to produce cultured marble, then took a huge bank loan out to get a 2,500-square-foot warehouse and turn it into a marble factory.

I still had lots of work going on with roofing and lots of guys working for me, but this new business took all my focus and energy. I wasn't being a very attentive father, either. The nanny was watching Patrick all the time. I was working 24/7, going to AA meetings, and dating. That was how I was coping.

I eventually brought in a second nanny because I just wasn't home that often. These were young girls that came over from different countries and wanted an opportunity in America. It was cheap to have them come and live in your house and take care of things. The family man had gone somewhere.... He just left.

I picked up a big contract to put sinks and tub surrounds in a development and hired a crew to do the installation. It was looking good, going along as planned. However, roofing was beginning to suffer due to my lack of interest in it, and the guys were screwing up jobs, costing me money. The contractors were starting to doubt me. They were not getting the attention they needed. We had this one huge development where seven roofs got screwed up. Every one of those roofs had to be paid for. That whole crew had to be let go just to save face with the contractor. He still wanted me, but I thought my future was in the marble. In time I lost all of his work. I was downsizing considerably in the roofing business—I didn't want to do roofing anymore, period. I began my decline by selling off equipment and getting rid of people, keeping just a small crew of maybe five to seven guys working.

Somewhere around this time, my brother Tim had come to visit me. He lived in Oklahoma, and they were feeling the recession there. He came down to see if there was opportunity for his company and if his family would like the area. He was in the heating and air-conditioning business. There was no doubt in my mind that he would thrive in South Florida, but he loved it in Oklahoma, and just didn't get that feeling of home in Delray.

It was good he came so I could show him what I had accomplished. Tim was my oldest brother. He was the one always trying to steer me in the right direction. I had made some real changes in my life since last seeing him. I can only hope I made him proud.

22

Bottoming Out

Things were changing too rapidly. I had taken on too much marble work and let roofing go by the wayside. I was getting further into debt each and every week, having to borrow more money, this time from a friend, just to purchase the supplies to produce the marble for work that was in progress. I was making money, but it was just disappearing into a huge pit.

One Sunday morning, it was just me and Patrick at the house. My debt had become totally unbearable. Bills were coming in. Huge amounts of money were owed, and I was falling apart. That day I felt a lot like when I went into detox. I couldn't get a handle on my emotions. It was very hard to put one foot in front of the other and trudge through this mind-blowing financial mess.

My world had totally fallen apart. Patrick was running around. At this time he was about three years old. I was in the kitchen, in a very bad mental state. I picked up a butcher knife, put it up against the wall with the blade sticking out, leaned up against it, and envisioned thrusting my body into it. I thought this would end my misery.

I was contemplating this and listening to Patrick playing. The thought of me doing this and him there and how this would affect his life was more powerful than my selfish need to end my misery. Sanity returned. I knew I was in big trouble and needed help.

I made a call to my mom, asking her to come and take care of Patrick. I didn't feel comfortable just leaving him with his nannies—I was in real mental turmoil, and I wanted family there taking care of him. There was no doubt Mom loved him, and I really needed her support. She flew right down.

After Mom arrived, I went over to Jim Bryant's house, the owner of the Beachcomber. It was night. He was pleased to see me and asked me in. We sat down in the living room. The summer Olympics were on TV. At first maybe he thought I was just visiting; however, after getting a good look at me, he asked, "What's wrong? You don't look so good."

I proceeded to tell him what was going on with me, telling him about the knife and my debt. He could see the catatonic state of mind I was in. He told me to go home, pack a bag, and come back. I told him I couldn't afford to go through treatment. He said, "You helped so many people that it's your turn to receive some help. Money isn't an issue. Now, go pack a bag." That's what I did. All along I was hoping that he would take me into treatment. I needed the escape. Mom took Patrick to her home in Pennsylvania while I was there.

My life was so pressured that I felt the relief right

away. My self-pity took the form of anger towards God for letting me fall on my face, and self-loathing as a failure. Thank God nobody else saw me that way. I got a lot of positive reinforcement from people who really knew me and loved me. But nonetheless, I still had to deal with me. No easy task, I assure you.

Treatment was very different this time, being sober and very familiar with the program. I was able to talk about myself and what was going on. I even told them about the affair. No secrets.

But I was an angry lad. One day in group, the subject of God had come up. It was probably a setup for me. To the group, I said, "If God was in this room right now, I would stand up and punch him right in the face." The counselor saw that as an opening to keep on me with my anger. I just kept going on and on about how angry I was about how things turned out. I purged every bit of anger in me that day. It seemed like I needed to see just how much I was blaming God for everything. I guess, if anybody can take my blame and anger, God can.

See, I think before, God was just saving my life. This time, he was saving my soul. This was a huge turn around in my progress. From this time on, I was much more focused on listening and caring about everybody else in there. I don't mean I took the focus off me, but I felt more responsible for reaching out to other people. The first time, I found my

82

healing in gratitude to God for giving me a new life. This time, I found my healing in loving others.

Helping others became a clear choice. It was where God was leading me. My gratitude came back. I could see how blessed I really was—not with houses and cars and all the material things of this world, but with the humility to stay away from a drink or a drug. With care and compassion for another suffering person. With honesty and trust. I was such a different person. I was even proud to be who I was. I had no regrets for anything that had happened in the past. I could see how my experiences could help others.

Up until this point, I saw myself through assuming eyes. Assuming how my father wanted me to be. I guess that came from my low self-worth. I was always worried about how people saw me, and I always had to be number one, whether it was being as bad as I could or being as good as I could. This was right there for me to see now.

I finally dealt with the guilt of leaving my father to die in the hospital, never to see him again, and feeling like the biggest loser a father could have as a son. It was all just a tool I used in my subconscious to feel sorry for myself.

Now I needed to say good-bye.... Dad had been close to me ever since he passed, but it was time for me to move on. I knew he was very proud. I closed my eyes and I could see him smiling at me. "Rest In Peace, Dad, I have it from here."

23

Closing Down Florida

I went into treatment angry at God and not wanting anything to do with his special life. I came out three weeks later feeling like my whole existence had become one great big blessing.

After returning home, I began to make a lot of changes in my life. The Beachcomber had set up a place for me to move into, a halfway house. I was given an apartment to live in with Patrick, and in return I ran a group two nights a week. From there I cleaned house with everything that was pulling me down. I put all my furniture in a storage unit, took my car and extra truck to the finance company and just told them, "Here." My credit was still perfect to this point, but I put a lot of marks on it that week. My serenity and sobriety were more important than a credit report. I got lucky with the marble company. Judy, the friend who helped me get sober in the beginning, knew somebody who was interested in it. I met with him, and he bought everything. I took a huge hit, but it did not matter. My debt was way bigger than I could get out of anyway. All I could do was recoup what I needed to survive.

I kept a small crew working in roofing, just for a job to do and money, but my heart and drive for it never really came back. I was going to a lot of AA meetings, working, and spending time with Patrick, just enjoying a little peace in my life.

Around that time, I received a phone call from Jeff, which was not unusual, as we always kept in touch with each other. However, this time was different. He called me to tell me he had H.I.V. At first I didn't believe him, shocked by the news. I questioned him on how he knew and how did that happen. I didn't know him to be an IV drug user. Both Steven and I were, but Jeff was always against that. He said he started right after I left. He even remembered the exact time it happened. He got real sick immediately and then it went away. AIDS was a new virus at that time. If you were an IV drug user, you were at high risk for it.

It was clear to me what my father had meant in the dream when he said: "Just get away, and get away now." Steven, Zowie, and I all went together to get tested. We were all clean.

I lived in that halfway house for six months. It was a real good time. I was able to share who I was and help a lot of guys in their sobriety. This was such a comfortable place for me to be, because when you share your life with somebody, it gives them an opportunity to get a sense of "I am not alone." It helps a person to accept where they are in life and to begin to change it from a place of acceptance.
From there, I moved into a three-bedroom

apartment. I still worked with the guys in the halfway house, but it was time for my life to go on. I had a small roofing crew, a girlfriend, and an Austrian nanny named Elizabeth.

I was living a good life on the inside as well as the outside. I felt free and at peace. Not all that committed to my girlfriend or to work, I was just waiting for the next stage of my life. It went on like this for about a year. I had gotten a new girlfriend because the last one was starting to resent me for not wanting the relationship she wanted. The next one pretty much went the same way. Work was like that, too. The guys wanted me to get bigger and grow, but I didn't want to and I didn't seem to care, either. It seemed like people who wanted something from me and were not getting it resented me. I could not be somebody I didn't want to be.

One weekend, I took my new girlfriend to the Bahamas. I loved it there. This trip was more for me than it was for us. It was a real romantic place, and we had a little hut on the beach. We went out to nice dinners and spent time together, but I was there to do some soul-searching for myself. One morning I got my snorkeling gear on and walked out into the water and swam around the island, just exploring. The ocean and I were good friends. I always got a sense of empowerment from it.

That weekend, I decided to move to Wilkes-Barre, Pennsylvania. My mom lived there in the house she grew up in. My plan was to go to school and pursue a career in alcoholism counseling.

Upon returning from our weekend in the Bahamas, I told everybody what I was going to do. My relationship, of course, came to an end. She was very upset and told me how selfish I was. You know, I was being selfish, but I don't think it was in a bad way. I had been married, and when I was, it was for real and forever. I wasn't emotionally shut down or guarded towards women. I was a lot of fun, and I was there to listen if needed. But, it was a lifetime of dreams crushed when my marriage went bad, and I just was not going back there. To me, that seemed perfectly logical.

Then there was Elizabeth, Patrick's nanny. I gave her the option of finding another family to work for or come with us. She chose to come. I think she saw it as an adventure. She was all in.

Next was work. I gave everything to Scott, my foreman. He just kinda stepped into my life there: apartment, furniture, household goods...everything. You might say he was happy to see us leave. We worked out a financial agreement, but I never saw one dime. Doesn't matter. I didn't care. I packed everything I could on the back of my truck, and off we went. It was September 1989. I was 30 years old and seven years sober.

24

Pennsylvania

The ride to Pennsylvania was pretty uneventful. It was a 25-hour trip from Boynton Beach to Wilkes-Barre, and I drove it straight through, stopping only for food and bathroom. This made the last leg of the trip a real struggle. However, entering Pennsylvania, the beauty of the rolling hills and the farmland was almost majestic. It was like we were being welcomed to their land. The mountains truly smiled at me and me back at them.

Now in PA, I took the GED test and passed, then signed up at the community college as a human services major. The staff at the Beachcomber thought I should pursue a career in alcoholism counseling. I agreed with them—helping people came naturally to me.

School was a whole lot easier than I had anticipated, probably due to all the reading I had done in recovery. I had gained an ease for school because of this discipline and was no longer the illiterate person of the past. It was a good feeling. I found that I was pretty intelligent.

I then became employed at an adolescent center for drug addiction and alcoholism. I started out as a technician on second shift. That included interacting with the kids as an authority figure, sharing experiences with them, taking them to meetings outside the facility, and charting their actions throughout the night. With the center's support, I earned the necessary credits and became a primary counselor. I was in charge of a portion of the clients, creating their treatment plans and setting up their after-care.

Moving on from there, I became a family counselor. During a client's stay, their family was required to attend a weekend at the facility. We provided education on alcohol and drug addiction as well as personal counseling sessions. I had three to four families there every weekend. This is probably the most important part of the program, especially with adolescents. My job was to bring them to a point of confrontation and help them deal with denial. I was very good at this, and I owe that to my conscious contact with God and allowing the Holy Spirit to be in charge.

Every weekend on my way to work I would clear my head and say a prayer that goes like this...

"God, I offer myself to Thee—to build with me and to do with me as Thou wilt. Relieve me of the bondage of self, that I may better do Thy will. Take away my difficulties, that victory over them may bear witness to those I would help of Thy Power, Thy Love, and Thy Way of life. May I do

90

Thy will always! AMEN"

This is a prayer from the third step of AA. It helped open my mind to more effectively deal with issues of the family weekends.

My personal life was pretty much the same as my work life. I was very active in AA and sponsored a lot of guys. This kept me close to my past. For an alcoholic, it is very easy to forget what it was like. Feel a little good...and you're off to the races again. Keeping your memory green is important. Working with others is very rewarding. It was a spiritually enlightening time of my life. Living under the guidance of the Holy Spirit, I was fearless. My relationship with my son was good. Life was good.

25

Patrick is Taken

Now life took a turn, like it always does. It has its way of teaching us new lessons...and mine was right around the corner.

Jolene had come to see Patrick a few times after we moved to PA. I guess she was trying to be a mother and maybe got some hopes on having a good life. She had moved to Buffalo, New York, and lived with a boyfriend. She was still drinking. She had stated she wanted to have Patrick once in awhile. I was not comfortable with that. He was only five years old and I did not trust her. I took him to New York a few times just to get used to her being in his life, but I never left him with her. The inevitable was coming, where I would have to let them have a relationship, but my insides were very much against it. Knowing the importance of having your mother in your life, I wanted nothing more for Patrick, but she was not right. However, I gave in.

One weekend she came and picked him up and took him to Buffalo. I went to New Jersey to visit my brother. Jolene and I were supposed to meet at a rest stop on the Garden State Parkway on Sunday evening. I got there on time, with the fear in my mind that they were not going to show. I kept chasing those thoughts out of my head, but as time went on,

I realized that they really weren't coming. Man, what do you do? My head was spinning. I kept trying to call her. No answer. I didn't know if they had gotten into an accident or she was playing games.

I drove home in despair. A friend came over to give me support and advice. Having still not heard from her, I called the police and asked them to go to her house. After a little while, I finally got a call from her. She told me she wasn't bringing him back and was filing for custody. Thank God I had good people in my life and they were able to keep me sane.

I decided to just go to Buffalo and take him back. Against their wishes, a few friends went with me, mainly to make sure I didn't do anything stupid. Upon arriving, I was met by her boyfriend. He called the police. They told me since I had no custody papers and we were not yet divorced, that she had every right to him and I could not take him. We went back to Pennsylvania and I filed for custody. She filed in New York. I had to get it thrown out in New York in order to fight for custody in Pennsylvania. That happened pretty fast, because Patrick had lived with me since he was born. The battle would be on my turf.

Jolene never wanted anything to do with being a mother before, so why now? He was not a trial-and-error toy. I hit her with everything I could. She not only didn't get custody, but she got all of her parental rights taken away. I knew everything about her and let her have it. I had everybody who knew her and/or me on my side. Now I just needed to get him back.

Well, she had taken off to Florida with him. I didn't know this at first. I just knew she wasn't bringing him back. I told her father if she showed up to let me know. He and I had a good relationship, and he knew she did not belong with Patrick. Several months went by and I received a phone call from her dad. He said, "I have him."

Jolene had gone to her father looking for help. He took Patrick and told her to leave. He said she was all messed up and he could not believe she had driven like that with him in the car. At that time, he had been so hurt by her that he wanted no more to do with her. It is very sad to see what this sickness can do to families. Bobby, her father, was always welcome in my home. He was a good man, and he loved Patrick very much and went out of his way to stay in his life.

Well, when I got that phone call, I went from the phone right to my car and drove 16 hours to where Bobby lived in Lakeland, Florida. It had been six months since I saw Patrick. He came running and jumped in my arms. I cried and hugged him for a long time. I stayed there overnight, and the next day we drove back to Pennsylvania. I finally had my boy back. Time to put this behind us.

26

WTF?

Bobby told me that while he was with him, Patrick was talking about sex a lot, and he was concerned about it. Once home, my Mom told me a few things he had said to her, too. Being a counselor myself, I thought I should get him some help and see what was going on. I got out the phone book found what I thought was children's counseling in our community. It turned out to be a community agency that investigated abuse in families. I didn't know this, and brought him there. We went in for our appointment, and I told the counselor everything about what had gone on and about the things he was saying, just being real open, figuring that's what you need if you are getting help. Well, she took him in a room, came out about a half hour later, and told me that she thought he was sexually abused. My stomach dropped. Then she told me that they suspected that I was the perpetrator, and that he was not allowed to leave with me and there had to be an investigation into the allegations.

I felt like I had a knife stuck into my stomach then turned upward with the blade shooting to my brain. Anger, fury. Cops show up and take me to the station for questioning. Guilty until proven innocent. I'm frantic about what is going on with my son and knowing they are totally looking at the wrong person.

When I was younger, I had a hatred that burned in me for the authorities. But let me tell you, I never hated like this before in my life. People have positions of authority that can just destroy others at the drop of a dime. I needed my program more than ever. I was so close to blowing that social office up on a daily basis. I envisioned it, planned it, everything. They attacked me as a father, I could not take care of my own son. They attacked my ego, what do people think of me? And they attacked my livelihood, I was a counselor that worked with kids. Let me tell you, the devil was doing some overtime to get me.

The investigation went on. Thirty days had passed. They wanted more time to prove my guilt. I was still not allowed to see Patrick. Another 30 days went by, and my lawyer said, "That's enough. They have overstepped their boundaries." He set up a meeting at the social office to see what evidence they had.

We went to this fucking place that I blew up, in my head, every day for two months. The caseworker took Patrick into a room. Me, my attorney, and the investigating officer went into another room where we could watch through a two-way mirror and listen. She then took out dolls and let him play with them. They were anatomically correct. What I saw almost made me throw up. He was playing with their private parts. Then she says to him, just like this, "What does daddy do?" Right at that statement I looked at my lawyer. He looked at me. We both knew she was

96

coaxing him to respond the way she wanted him to. The detective looked at both of us and said, "Come on, we are going in." I went right over to my son, picked him up, and said to her, "You are the one that should be arrested for child abuse and have your life destroyed because of it." My lawyer just told me to take him and go home. He would handle it from there.

I know bad things happen to people, and through those last eight months, Patrick and I had our share. But I want to say, staying angry about things only hurts you further, and I knew this first and foremost. At the time, I had to live my life in a forgiving way, just for my own sanity. I needed to view that lady as being very misguided in a screwed-up system. I could not afford the emotional turmoil something like this could produce. My priority through this was to stay clean in my heart as well as drug-free. I did not seek any type of restitution or satisfaction in going back after these people. I was just glad to get my little boy back and get him some real help.

I did get Patrick the help he needed, and I also got the help I needed, because all of this did damage to both of us. It turned out that he had never been abused. He had been through a lot, the doctor said. Somewhere along the line, he had seen more than he should have. But he was just reaching out in this way for attention. Finally, after all my son and I had been through, our lives took a turn towards peace and fulfillment.

The devil that chases me will lose every time. God has assured me a special life, and I will not be denied it.

27

Visiting Jeff

Jeff had called me. It was just before my ninth anniversary of being sober. I remember that clearly, because I spoke of him at my celebration. He asked me to come visit him. He didn't think he had much time left, and wanted to see me. This would be the first time I had seen him since my last drink, when my brother took me out of that bar and brought me to detox. It had been almost nine years. We had talked numerous times on the phone, but I was never really comfortable going back to the old neighborhood.

When I arrived, Jeff's appearance was shocking. He was extremely skinny. All of his bones were visible. He was very frail and weak. My memories were of a bigger, stronger, and better-looking Jeff. My heart was softened and saddened. We sat for hours talking over old times.

One time, we went to Atlantic City on a drunken binge. We drank and hit a few casinos. When we were ready to leave, we didn't remember where we started. We had no idea where we left the van. Instead of looking for it, we just kept partying and gambling. We were always very lucky.

It goes back to that old saying, "God watches out for babies and drunks." We partied through to the next night, came out of a bar, and there was our van.

Another time we went down there and played blackjack all night. I couldn't lose. I ended up winning $2,500. We went home, bought a bunch of cocaine, and an old 18-foot boat. It held its own stories of partying for nights to come.

There was another time, when we were drinking in the woods by Campbell's Junction. It was just the two of us. A cop was out on the road. His lights were on, and he was dealing with some issue out there. We decided to pick up this huge rock—it took both of us to lift it—and we threw it through his windshield and took off running. The cop shot at us. When we stopped running, Jeff realized that a bullet had grazed his side. That was just like him. He always got all the bad luck out of the things we did.

He told me about Peter, his younger brother. Peter had been beaten over the head and left to die in the crow weeds. He said he also had AIDS, but he was killed before the AIDS got him. His older brother, Richard, had died. He too had AIDS. We sat and watched a video of Richard that was made for AIDS education. He told me Steven was in jail again. I guess he had relapsed. I don't remember. Michael was still doing good and staying sober.

Towards the end of the night he told me, "Pat, I have to show you something. This is why I really had to see you." He put a video in the VCR and turned it on. It was of a bunch of us partying in his kitchen with a quarter barrel in the sink. We were all drinking and having a good old time. He pointed out everybody, one by one, and told me how they had died. He said: "Everybody in this video is dead but you and me, and I am about to die. You made the right choice, Pat."

We parted shortly after that. He said to me, "You probably won't see me anymore." The way he said it still sticks in my mind. It was with great strength and courage. I left there very emotionally drawn out, silent, and in tears.

Jeff went home about a month later. I say that because that's what he told me—"I'm going home."

"GOING HOME"

To return to a place of pure abandonment. To be as innocent as a newborn baby. To be pure in spirit. To surrender completely to a new beginning. After every emotional bottom in life, there is new birth on the other side. This is something that doesn't ever stop until our purpose is complete and we return home to be with our loved ones who have gone before us. Forgive your past. Be free to share it with others, so they too can be free.

"Sleep well, my friend"

THE BEGINNING

About me, the author:

This story began over 40 years ago. I'm 53 years old now and Patrick is 27. I have since remarried and raised four children; three boys and my youngest, a girl. I have lived a whole other life since that time, with a lot of ups and downs. I still feel extremely blessed to have made it past the age of 23. One of my favorite statements is: "But for the grace of God, there go I."

The people in my life are my support system. They are important to my spiritual being and I need to keep them close to me.

Patrick J. Doty

When Enough is Enough

Do not fight this soul sickness alone. Call Alcoholics Anonymous / Narcotics Anonymous intergroup in your local area. They are listed in your phone book and are more than willing to help. Helping you is how each and every one of them survives.

Maybe you, or a loved one, aren't ready today. It's never too early to do a little research. Find a local Alcoholics Anonymous phone number, write it down, and put it in your wallet. This way, when you are ready, help is a phone call away.

Made in the USA
Lexington, KY
01 December 2012